101 IDEA FOR BOOSTING SALES OF YOUR HANDMADE ITEMS

CHECKLIST

NATALIA SHMAKOVA

101 idea for boosting sales of your handmade items

Checklist

Natalia Shmakova is an established Russian author and experienced entrepreneur running her own business since 2009. In this book she offers you a ready solution to boosting sales of handmade items despite the recent economy stagnation. The sales figures for handmade items have significantly dropped last year. Prospective clients are saving money and only buying the essential things. A huge number of beautiful high quality works have flooded the market.

Craftsmen need to put a lot more effort in their works to be noticed. This book contains useful recommendations on the successful usage of the 10 main sales channels. By pinpointing each of the 100 steps in this checklist you will become the bestselling artist in your area of competence. The main goal of this book is to help you to focus on the most important actions with the best outcome to save your time and efforts.

https://www.etsy.com/shop/FeltFashionmagazine
https://www.facebook.com/natalia.shmakova.16

Contents

Check your website and Etsy store

Review the relationship with your customers

Check your Instagram

Check your social media accounts

Review the range of your shop

Assess the quality of photos of your merchandise

Classical and fashion marketing

Networking

Personal effectiveness

Promote your personal brand

Check your website and Etsy store:

1

Is there a nice banner containing the name of your shop and a hint at what you do? Is it still the right fit or a bit outdated?

2

Is there a good quality personal photo on the avatar of your shop? It is always better when it shows you in it, not the logo or a fluffy cat pic.

3

Make sure you use your name and surname in your shop's name or description. It is also beneficial if the name of your shop contains your own name and the description of what you actually do. For example, Jane Smith, jewellery design.

4

Take stylish and good quality pictures of your designs. Check the background of your photos. It should either be nice or just plan white. The visual content on your shop page creates the mood and either attracts customers to your works or pushes them away. Create and present a whole look when inviting someone to model your creations. The main photo should be bright and catching the eye. There should also be some close-ups and pictures presenting the real size of the items for sale. Do not use cheap mannequins and try to make sure there are no such details in the background like power sockets and crumpled bedsheets!

5

Do not skip the "info" area (it can also be called "about us" or "about the author"). Write something nice about yourself like you would be introducing your good friend. A few examples of the questions you could answer in this article are: What do you do? How long have you been passionate about it? Whether or not you make your designs to order? What did you achieve in this field? What makes you proud? What inspires you? Who are your favourite customers?

6

Define the payment and delivery methods. Make sure the prices for your designs are clearly visible and easy to find.

7

Write detailed and emotional descriptions for your creations adding as much detail about the surface, colour and any special notes. Do not forget to define the measurements, give care instructions and add some advice on how to style the piece.

8

Use all of the tags available to you. This will make your work easier to find. Check what tags your colleagues use for the same types of creations. Add some seasonal and theme tags e.g. holidays, style, colour and shape, animals, type of materials used etc.

9

Draw your customer's attention to your other items adding the links to similar designs and styling opportunities in the description of your creation.

10

Regularly post updates on your blog writing about yourself, your work and showing behind the scenes you the processes in your workshop. This helps to build your own brand for the future clients.

Review the relationships with your clients:

11

Collect information about your customers e.g. mail and phone numbers, some valuable information like birthdays, hobbies, names and age of children (whenever appropriate).

12

Keep in touch with your clients on a regular basis. Tell them about promotions and events, send personal promotional coupons. Send your congratulations to their birthdays and national holidays.

13

It is always easier to sell repeatedly to a well known customer than to find a new one. Send the information about your new in items to your clients.

14

Write thank you letters to your new clients. Ask them whether everything is all right with the item and if they are happy with the purchase.

15

Collect feedback. Ask every customer to leave you a note about their experience and add the feedback to your social media.

16

Think who your customer is. What do your best 3 clients have in common? There can be a couple of different "portraits" for different types of goods you are selling.

17

The most valuable thing is a chance to personally meet your customer. A chat with a client helps to define HOW and WHY they are making their decisions. What else they would like? What was missing? If they are not buying then why is that? Use every chance to speak with your audience.

18

Pay attention to the way of life of your best clients. What is their educational level? Personal values? Average income? Friends? This information will give you a hint on where to look for prospective clients offline.

19

Make nice small gifts that would make your clients smile. People will be happy to purchase from you again.

20

Clients can be everywhere. Always have your business cards and promotional brochures with you. Use every opportunity to tell about yourself and your creations.

Check your instagram account:

21

The pictures should be sharp, bright and catching the eye. It is beneficial to have a uniform feed colour scheme and a common idea behind all the photos.

22

Add keywords (footwear for example if you are producing footwear) to your nickname, name and profile description. Make the description very clear and answering one main question: What is this profile about?

23

Posting 1 to 2 photos a day would be optimal to stay in your customer's feeds.

24

Add some personal pictures and behind the scenes in between the photos of your designs.

25

Add descriptions to your photos. Tell funny stories, describe the items and speak about your life. Always mention price in the description.

26

Be nice to your customers, send them likes for their likes and always answer all the comments.

27

Keep an eye on the emerging new and popular hashtags that you might use. Add those to your posts. Like other people's posts with these hashtags.

28

Create videos and stories. They always catch a lot of attention. You can either film those in advance or use Instagram's own tools and create content on the go.

29

Try to interact with your customers. Ask them to like your pictures, ask questions and make them leave comments.

30

Organise giveaways and quiz nights. Try to arrange guest posting on other accounts with similar audiences.

Check your social media accounts:

31

Start your accounts on the most popular social media like Facebook, Twitter, Tumblr or Pinterest. Start a YouTube channel. Let's assume you're already on Instagram.

32

Think of short and nice nicknames. Add keywords to the profile description. Use the same style for all the headers/avatars on all social media accounts. Add FAQ's and discussions. Add links to your personal website or blog.

33

Write a few words about yourself and add the project description. Create a nice presentation for your project or designs and publish it everywhere you think it might be useful.

34

Fill your accounts with interesting content. Add personal photos and information about yourself along with pictures of your designs. Be honest and open-minded, this will gain you trust. Show how you create your items. Post customer's pictures showing your designs and people's feedback. Share useful information on how to care for the items they bought, give some advice on gaining max value out of your creations. Sprinkle it all with some funny pictures and stories.

35

Create short branded videos. The most popular content of this kind are short funny videos and talking advice. People are happy to share those. Live talk sessions are a good way to catch attention of your customers. Don't be shy to organise those.

36

Organise giveaways, polls and debates, throw in provocative themes and discussions, try to interact with your audience.

37

Make promotional offer or publish a coupon. This kind of content is often reposted, so it is a perfect chance to boost your sales.

38

Use the "star feedback". If a media person or a content creator mentions your items in their account it creates a blast of sales.

39

Use the https://smmplanner.com to manage the publications in your accounts.

40

Create pictures and texts for your posts in advance. Choose one day a week and dedicate it to writing content. Smmplanner lets you plan and develop a posting plan for your content. Make series of nice pictures on occasions and going on a holiday to a nice place.

Review your stock:

41

Your product range should contain 3 categories of goods. 1. A best selling product - a basic item under 10$ that triggers spontaneous purchases. 2. The middle segment - your main designs. 3. Something expensive to boost your own status.

42

Analyse what people do buy from you most. Focus on this product or service. Think how you could add more positions to this sector of the range. A famous designer usually creates his works keeping his customers in mind. Always think what your clients need. Nowadays it is very important to create what people need and want to buy and follow the trends. Be careful trying to create something that nobody else does. Some items have very low margins and some are just something nobody needs so this might be the reason why nobody else is producing those.

43

Make something that your friends could buy. At least you will always be able to sell it to them.

44

Follow the mass market ideas. People are not ready to pay 1000$ for items of an unknown designer.

45

There are 3 elements of a well balanced collection. These are:
The base: a couple of hits that do not change significantly in every new season.
The middle: items retaining the same shape but constantly being adopted to new trends. Use new colours, fabric or prints to be
The top: the most trendy items attracting the most attention to your store. These should compliment the goods from the other levels of your stock pyramid and add energy to the looks.

46

Statistically speaking, 75% of the items in your shop should be the ones you can easily sell. These are the basic ones. 15% of all the stock can follow trends. New experimental designs should take only 10% of the whole lot.

47

Optimise the size range if producing clothes. Define your target audience and make a research what sizes are more popular amongst it. Focus on those figures..

48

The price of an item is in direct connection with its "perceived value". If you produce interesting designs and the quality of your items is better than everything your competition can offer, your prices can also be higher than average. Just do not forget that your items cost exactly as much as your customers are willing to pay for them. Here are 2 tips from Gosha Rostovshtshikov, chief buyer at Harvey Nichols, Baku: (49,50)

49

There is a huge deficit in women's plus size market. You can make real money producing basic good quality items. Though this doesn't count for fantasy designs.

50

Remember: information is money. The more you tell what "virgins" have sewn and "goats" have knitted the better. Tell stories about your product, but make sure they sound interesting! Why is it so different, what makes it special, what is it made of, how long have you been drawing your designs and what inspired you to create this piece?

Assess the pictures of your items:

51

I always say that pictures are the main sales channel on the Internet. Everything depends on their quality! All other efforts will result in nothing if you have bad quality pictures of your items.

52

It should straight away be clear what item in the picture is for sale. Make sure the customers can get an idea of the real size of an item just looking at the photo.

53

If you haven't got any professional equipment, take all the pictures in the soft daylight. You can catch it on a cloudy day when no straight sunlight peers through the clouds. The best spots for an improvised photo shoot are outside or on the window sill.

54

Background is also very important. Do not take your pictures too close to a wall making the picture divided by a wall skirt and the wall. Other examples of bad backdrops are: patchy background (like carpets), walls with distracting elements like sockets, light switches, pictures etc., curtains, crumpled bedsheets and cheap mannequins. Good spots to make your pictures are: in the street, in front of a neutral backdrop, in a special light box, in a studio, in front of a nice backdrop that complements the item you are trying to sell, in a street cafe, in a nice interior etc. Use aperture controls if you know how to do that to achieve blurry background.

55

Create a whole look and mood. If someone is modelling your designs make sure to find matching shoes and add nice makeup and hairstyle. Try to catch live pictures in motion. The customer should want to be in the place of that model. Or to possess that beautiful things presented in the picture.

56

Learn the composition and golden ratio basics. Put objects in the natural view flow points on the intersection of the grid lines. Remember to keep the horizon straight and try to keep it up with the upper or lover line in the grid.

57

Learn how to use a photo editor. Cropping, exposure fixes and adding text and watermarks, retouching, background blur should become your best friends.

58

Every artwork is special, but there are some areas with the most interesting details. Take pictures of that part from all possible angles. Highlight the texture, make sure the light is enhancing the details and deepening the shadows where needed.

59

Put your camera at the same level with the items or a bit lower while taking pictures. This will make your items look bigger and more convincing. While working with items for sale I am trying to create unique atmosphere that could enhance them. Ideally I am trying to make a piece of art even out of very common things. (Renee Aylworth)

60

It is the pictures that can turn your item into a piece of art. Bad pictures make perfect artwork look like cheap stuff from mass market shops.

Classical and fashion marketing:

61

Always offer matching accessories and additional items that would go well with your pieces. Add links to those matching items on the page of your main item. Make a good offer. The main rule to make the scheme work is: the client pays less for bulk buys.

62

Offer alternatives if you do not have the exact match. Suggest to buy more for the husband, mum etc. Make offers to those who wanted to buy and cancelled last minute.

63

Offer a risk free deal: a chance to try the piece on before buying or to return it without explanation.

64

Do not be afraid to raise the price by 10-20%. It isn't so important for the customers, but can make a huge difference for you.

65

Make special offers and invitation only sales for your customers. Tell them what's new in your store. Repeat sales is one of the main marketing tools. Are you congratulating your clients on their birthday? Are you calling them half a year later to find out how they are doing? It is just a matter of good manners to offer to renew the item they bought.

66

Find out what makes your items unique. Why are they different from similar items on the market? What unique value are you offering to your clients? Do your customers know about it? Do you tell them about it?

67

Use events marketing to your advantage. Tea parties, friendly chatting, theme evenings and workshops - there are plenty of reasons to host a party and gain new clients.

68

Ask your customers to tell their friends about you. Collect feedback. How do you know the customer was happy? How do you keep in touch with him after the sale was wrapped up?

69

The classical fashion marketing means creation of new collections following set deadlines. Showtime. Working with buyers, collecting individual orders, end of season sale. Start working on the winter collection in summer and vice versa. This will help you to be ready for the season when it starts. It is easier to take pictures of a whole series of pieces. If you are hiring a photographer and a model and renting a studio, it makes sense to take pictures of at least 7-10 of your items at once. By the end of the season assess your items and think whether they will still be trendy next season. If the answer is no, significantly cut the prices and put the items on sale by the end of the season.

70

If you decided to take part in a runway show you will need models. Find a local platform where you can hire a model for free of very cheap. Tell the exact size and height of the models, date, time, place and the number of people you need. Look for models working on their portfolio and ready to model for pictures in return. Discuss in advance what kind of hairstyle, shoes and basic clothes they will need. Another way is to find out the sizes and bring shoes for the models. Ask the sponsors whether there will be makeup and hair stylists or you should invite your own. Choose music for your show. Established fashion houses get music made to order for their shows. You are violating copyrights by using modern popular tracks. It isn't as critical for small local events. If you are worried about the copyright issues, go for classical music. It is always the right choice.

Organise professional video and photo shoot for your show. Ask the photographer to make backstage shoots and take some pictures of the models after the show.

Felt Fashion Show 2013

(Saint-Petersburg, Russia)

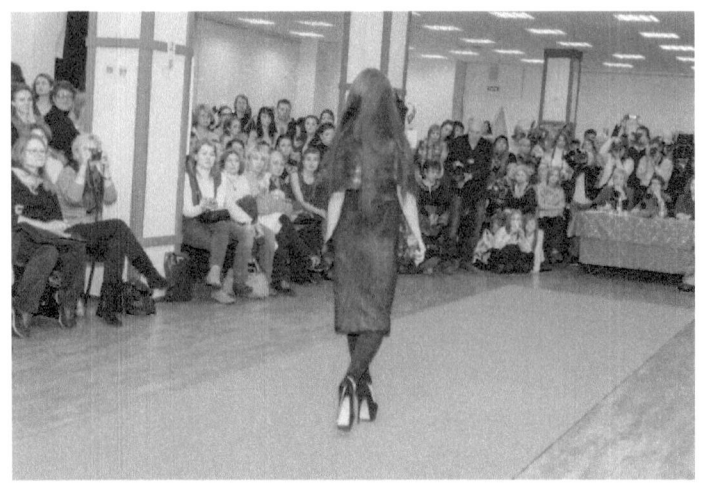

Choose your friends. Networking

71

The money you make are the average level of the income of 5 of your closest friends. This doesn't mean you have to abandon your loved ones if you are not happy with your income. Just try to widen your network. Search for leaders and people who already achieved the level you are aiming for. Find a reason to meet them. Just do not intervene in their private space.

72

Your network is not only built of people you are communicating with in real life. People, whose books you read are also part of your circle and are affecting you. Carefully filter the books, films, news and feeds. There is enough garbage in there.

73

Help people finding each other. If you have contacts of good experts, share them. If you feel two people could be useful for each other, connect them. If you can help, do help others. There is a useful tool: give others something that you would like to get. If you want more sales, help someone to sell something. If you want more money, think carefully and donate money to a charity.

74

If there are any clients that you do not like working with, just stop it. If these are your relatives, try minimising the time you spend together and do not mention the topics you both do not agree on.

75

Write a list of people (relatives, friends, clients) that boost your mood and inspire you. Make sure you contact with them more. Work on these relationships. Find a way to thank them for being part of your life.

76

Learn to tell about yourself and what you are doing in a minute. Precise and emotional to make sure you can interest people with your ideas. Practice in front of a mirror.

77

Always carry business cards and leaflets with you. Potential clients can be everywhere. Ask for a permission to leave a couple of your business cards in a hair saloon, dental practice, in a nail studio and ask to recommend you whenever possible.

78

Make alliances with colleagues. It is always easier to organise events or projects together. Collaborate with people from similar niches. If you are making scarves, for example, then look for someone making hats or brooches. You can promote your items together, because you all have similar audiences. Print a joint leaflet. Book a common exhibition space. Write posts about each other on your social media.

79

Find a fashion blogger creating the kind of content you like. Give him or her some of your items as a present. If the item is expensive, discuss a test-drive. Let the blogger wear the piece and ask him/her to write about this experience on their blog. You can use the same approach when working with fashion stylists.

80

Collaborate with small niche shops. If you sell bags, scarves or hats, it is useful to become friends with a shoe or outerwear store. Same rules apply for online shops. If you are selling jewellery try making friends amongst beauty studios.

Personal effectiveness

81

Avoid the burnout syndrome. Do not do things you do not want to do. When you are creating things you like, time flies and you are getting more and more energy. At the end you are tired, but happy with the work you have accomplished. Leave all the things you do not like to do to others. If it is impossible, cut them in 15-minute intervals to make sure you wont get tired. Plan your time off. Make yourself a proper day off every week. Do something you like, go new places, treat yourself and do not switch on the computer, tv and phone on that day.

82

Write a to do list the day before. Make long lists for the whole week. Try arranging 3-5 things to do for a single day. If something requires a lot of your attention then plan only that one thing for the day.

83

Start your day with the most difficult task or something very important, but not too inspiring.

84

Buy yourself additional time. Let freelancers do the jobs you do not want to do. Find the right people on peopleperhour.com

85

Do not force yourself to do things you are too lazy to do. Laziness indicates useless work. It is either not your work or just not the right time to do it. However, if you feel lazy to do anything at all it is a good reason to seek psychological advice.

86

While writing plans make sure you pay enough attention to the main things you have to do. Put urgent non important things towards the end of the list. Do those if there will be time left to work on those. Or just delegate to others. Cross out non urgent and not important tasks straight away.

87

Automate everything you can. Especially your mailing list. Use sendpulse.com to send up to 15.000 emails for free just in 1 click.

88

Charge your "batteries" by taking a break every 1,5 hours. Make one day a family day and do not work. Go visit new places.

89

Follow a healthy work-life balance and do sports. Do not forget about a healthy diet.

90

Read my book "Time management for handmaders" and do exercises from that book. This will help you to successfully prioritise your interests following your values.

Managing your personal brand

90

Write books. It is not as hard as it might seem. Books will instantly award you an expert status. There are a couple of ways of doing it quickly. In the modern world you do not have 10 years to write a book. The algorithm is easy: send audio copies of your seminars and workshops to freelancers to decipher. Edit the text you get or send it to a professional editor. Find good quality pictures. Your book is ready.

Then there are some variations:

A) Publish the book yourself. Any publishing house could do that. You can always find money to publish the book on a crowdfunding platform. Just make a good presentation of your project and upload it to the site. Then tell about it on all your social media.
B) Send the manuscript to a couple of publishing houses. They will edit and print

the book. The only downside to the whole story is that you barely earn anything.
C) Send the book to an online publishing house. Professional editors will edit your book and put it on Amazon. So you will earn money from each sale the book makes.

92

Find your uniqueness. What makes you different from other people in your field? What could you offer to others? What are you doing to make other people's lives easier? What builds your public image? What is your X-Factor? Your ability to add value to items. In other words, your ability to do more than anyone else for your clients and keep this standard consistently high.

93

Put accent to your lifestyle. Actively chat with your followers, post cool pictures showing your life from different angles, share your philosophy. Everybody sees the world different. It is very interesting to see it through yours. What you see as something ordinary might be extremely interesting for others. Share the beauty you have inside. Create your own world in your works and around you and let the followers have a sneak peek inside it.

94

Take part in exhibitions and fashion shows. This makes your brand recognised and creates new contacts.

95

Speak on conferences, live chats and online events.

96

Continue studying and learn every day. Follow tendencies and new trends. Keep an eye on the changes in your niche. Put together a plan of your additional education. Learn from the best.

97

Find online publics and meet people doing same thing as you. Share and discuss information with them. Compliment other artists on their achievements and organise events together. No one can achieve success on his own.

98

Find a tutor who already succeeded in your niche. Try to become friends and offer him something useful. Analyze and copy his strategies. Try to get into his network and find out who his tutors are.

99

Remember, your reputation is how you get on with the others. Your way of communication shows your inner world. Always be polite.

100

Find a couple of your favourite and most effective ways of marketing, something that works for you. Concentrate 80% of your efforts on those. Remember the Pareto rule. 20% of your efforts bring 80% of success. The main question is to find the right 20%. This rule works in every part of your lives and can be used for various situations.

101

Your business, your art and handmade represents and reflects you. It is your mirror. If you grow, your works do also grow.

I wish you happiness and growth in your chosen field. May the creation process bring you joy.

Natalia Shmakova, Entrepreneur, mon of 3, founder of Felt Fashion magazine and the international felt exhibition "The new life of traditions", author of the "Antology of designer felt" book.
https://www.amazon.com/dp/B01FCDA4YG

I love to travel around the world, create new projects. And also felt crazy wool hats.

My book about felting will soon be out.

www.ingramcontent.com/pod-product-compliance
Lightning Source LLC
Chambersburg PA
CBHW021309240526
45463CB00019B/2818